Published by: Joe Prisk

Book Design by: Jason D. McIntosh

ISBN: 979-8-218-73661-3 (Softcover)
ISBN: 979-8-218-73662-0 (eBook)

THROUGH
the Years

Poems of Love, Faith, and Growth

By Joe Prisk

DEDICATION

This book of poems is dedicated to the Author of all love and understanding – Jesus the risen Christ.

I also wish to thank my wife, Patti and my children, Chris and Brae who inspired these poems.

Enjoy the read and be blessed.

"...For love is from God and everyone who loves is born of God and knows God."

I John 4:7 (The Holy Bible)

PART ONE

1972–1973

RETROSPECT

Tonight again I've seen
    that fair red hair
    appearing to me
    as if out of nowhere
Feelings stirred again
    as I sat near
    to the one that held
    my heart while here
With her I felt
    so light, so free
    between us now
    an empty that leaves me
Standing cold, alone
    not complete somehow
    but when will I again see
    that red hair?
        for now
She leaves again
    to where she came
    and I go back
    to where I was;
    my head in the sky.

1972

aside, alone

a stone curved
and shaped
can still not feel

aside, alone
is a stone

a heart cold
and closed
can not exist

aside, alone
is this stone

a love crushed
and tossed away
still hurts inside

aside, alone
is my stone

1972

first snow

first snow
  delicate foe
    to we who live
      in gutters

frosted clown with little joy
fresh garbage tinsel reflects little light
my only friends fill my frozen shoes
empty bottles strain a jolly merry
in garbled tones to my running nose
naked evergreens are thrown among us
presents of past years
share a seat at our christmas feast
I melt away with the fading ho-ho-ho's
and kiss the cobblestones
goodnight

wind blow
  let me know
    if I will live
      to see another
first snow

1972

reflections

it hurts even more
to die in rain
the drops join tears
wasted members of the corp
blood gets diluted
flowing, dispersing and leaving
red food among blue sparkling

why go and die
there is always the meadowland
refuge for all
what of the putsch?
even now the buttercups
cast shell liners
daises await orders
to strafe the quiet grasslands
tiny laughing frogs
goose-step off to Poland
dragonflys pull levers
destroying innocent butterflies
and ignorant beetles
the characters change
but the lily pads still cast
green shadows on blue sparkling

(reflections continued)

the sun smells so warm
the corp shines so bright
each member in his own square
black/white
a few pawns are finding
discomfort in obeying commands
but they are the first to go anyway
tiny pebbles giving red food
to a lost world
in blue sparkling

1972

aftermath

Mary's smile has now been used
but her golden teeth
still reflect the tithe of the poor

frog prince and the sleeping virgin
have rushed to their cottage on Elbe
it will guarantee quiet
consummation must be done
darkness is the tradition
spent rice mingles in their hair
a touch of pagan
that upsets the holy dome

ceremonial slip
someone forgot to peel the onion
wasted water now lies
in the corner of the cottage suite
Venus has turned her back
and Mary remains fast asleep

1972

instead

the oak's coat has turned brown and red
  winter must be coming
look mommy the leaves they're dead
  winter must be coming
broken cradle - empty bed
  winter must be here
her youngest child was never fed
  winter must be here
the angels received - pity they said
  winter has come

I wish they'd taken me

instead

1972

autumn

*"For it is shame even to speak of the things that they do in secret;
but when anything is exposed by the light it becomes visible . . ."*

1

far from where I could imagine
stood a boy
caught in a fantasy that strangles innocence
but there was a calm
a tiny peace
with open arms and words that comforted
light as frost melting in the morn
warm as mom's glance on graduation day

2

the lights must be off
to do things better not seen
darkness has it's way of telling on you
halloween tricks
no treat for naughty ones
but even in autumn
there are breezes that refresh
and carry colors to paint the sky
soft as the wind
on my almost chilly cheeks

(autumn continued)

3

Tomorrow I'll find that mask
the one with my name scribbled inside
it stops me
from being understood when I talk
but I can stick my tongue out
the mouth hole
no one knows it's me
except my tongue
masks are fun for some
but there was always confidence
in eyes as red as mine
and on the back of labels
for prizes no one ever won
and give away toys
in boxes marked 'eat first'
strong arms to hold weak feet
above the flood

4

Running always hurts my eyes
as I cry for my feet
thinking always feels better
with my mind shut and my heart fixed
for keeps
when it's hard to move
your friends all stick with you
breath that can't meet

the morning freshness without crying
for the night before
autumn is only one season
and spring is for the growing
some eggs never hatch
and are lost under feathers that kill
but there
was the Light
loving me dirt and all
reaching into winter with spring
offering the warmth
to hatch my heart
singing from a cross
the sweetest lullaby
the air could hold

5

Presents are found in the strangest places
colored eggs under couches
and pretty dolls under trees
but I found mine hanging
bleeding in pain for me
reverse can be found
when your going down hill
if the right ONE shifts
and HE gave me Patti
soft as powder
and twice as sweet
to heal with me the autumns

1973

PART TWO

1986–1987

COME NOW

Come now
       write songs and laugh 'till five in the morning

Come now
    for I have overcome the world
    so that you can rest and enjoy

Come now
    fly kites with laughing children
    who couldn't care a lick for this world

Come now
    learn what it is to trust
    a Father who is faithful

Come now
    take a deep breath
    you've just begun to realize what truth is

       for birds don't look
       every time they leap

1986

An excerpt from
"The Hippopotamus" by T.S. Elliot:

"Flesh and blood is weak and frail
Susceptible to nervous shock;
While the True Church can never fail
For it is based upon a rock."

Oh fair bride
marred and shamed
painted greed green by idle talkers
and merchants in the court
Oh fair bride
tender and beautiful
wrestled and raped
by sweeties in wolves cloths
Oh fair bride
your prince comes
to spit upon the clay once more
so that blind eyes can see
His fair bride
in all her holy splendor
spotless, purged of all dross
   Did you get the invitation?

1987

AT CHRISTMAS TIME

"THEY'RE LOST - THEY'RE LOST"
    CRIED THE MAN
    PLEASE DON'T DISTURB
    THE PEOPLE SAID
    WHAT WE NEED IS A BETTER PROGRAM

"THEY'RE LOST - THEY'RE LOST"
    STILL HE CRIED
    WITH TEARS NOW ETCHING FROM HIS EYES
    YOU'RE MUCH TOO SERIOUS TO ENJOY
    AND THEY MADE HIM
    SIT IN THE BACK BY THE DOOR

"THEY'RE LOST - THEY'RE LOST"
    ONCE MORE CAME THE TONE
    LOST AND FOUND
    THAT'S THE SEXTON'S ROLL
    WE HAVE LONG SINCE CLOSED OUR EYES
    WE HEAR ONLY OUR OWN SELFISH CRIES

OUT INTO THE BATTLE THAT ONE MAN WENT
    THE FIRE DROVE THE PEOPLE TO REPENT
    A CROWN OF GLORY FOR ONE LIKE THIS
    A FATE OF JUDGEMENT FOR THOSE WHO MISSED
    THE CRY OF THE HERALD
        "THEY'RE LOST - THEY'RE LOST"

1987

TO ARTIST BROTHERS

we get so used to colored things
we forget there is white

we're so caught up in our own way
we forgot to think of what we say
to our own suffering we go
artists lost and poets none
into the goo called popularity

we cease to speak of anything
and merely show our emptiness
canvas blank as snow
hearts like searching rooms
we never found

But Rejoice, Oh Pilgrim Friend
when the Master kindly lends
a talent or two of Kingdom jewel
to proclaim the pure -
announce the right -
show forth our Creator
                white as light

1987

DON'T CARRY WHAT IS NOT YOURS

don't carry what is not yours
your arms are too small
your head is too big
your strength is dried up

don't carry what is not yours
your life is too fragile
your joy is too limited
your needs are too great

don't carry what is not yours
the day is too short
your heart is too unknown
your mystery still unfolds

don't carry what is not yours
there's another who will

1987

Christmas Presents

Christmas presents are large and small
brightly wrapped for show – ribbons tie all

some fill spaces in little children's eyes
some come from tradition
full of "I love you" lies
some block out the freshness of fallen snow
some take the place of
the blessed truth we know
some hang from dying trees
between the shining lights
some take and give nothing in return
causing bickering and fights

this present is none of the above
it is a small taste
            of a great love for you

1987

that's enough

happy is a small face
with eyes big enough
and lips soft enough
to complete my world
peace in a smile
with love that glows
and a heart that knows
God
that's enough

1987

I LOVE

I love
not because of who I am
but for the sake of time

I love
not because it is safe
but because it's all I know

I love
not because I couldn't lose my heart
but because I have one to lose

I love you
risky words in a risky world
of love

1987

brussel sprouts

I hate the taste of brussels sprouts
the taste is indescribable
like little cabbages
condensed down to little green balls
yuk!

but to sit with someone like you
even brussels sprouts
start to look good
not that good
but I've heard if you
put enough sugar on anything
it turns sweet
you are my sugar
and sitting across the table
from you
I think I could handle
anything
life serves me

1987

PART THREE

1987–2018

still my girlfriend

you are still my girlfriend
still the one
I hold hands with
still the one
I can't stop looking at
still my girlfriend

yes you have other titles
mother of my children
my blessed wife
but the one title
that continues to thrill me
is my girlfriend

how proud to walk besides you
how great to let others know
   you're with me
to kiss you is so fantastic

I've always dreamed
of having a girlfriend
   like you

1987

YOU'RE HERE

IN THE STILLNESS
   YOU'RE SO QUIET
IN THE MORNING LIGHT
   YOU'RE BEAUTIFUL
AND EVEN THOUGH MY MIND RACES
   I DON'T ASK THE QUESTIONS
   YOU'RE HERE

THE WORLD GOES ON IT'S WAY
   WE LAY TOGETHER HOLDING HANDS
QUIETLY THINKING
   WHAT'S IMPORTANT
LIKE FRESH FALLEN SNOW
   HOW BABIES GROW
AND EVEN THOUGH THIS WORLD
   HAS A MILLION QUESTIONS
   I DON'T NEED TO ASK
   YOU'RE HERE

AND WHEN LIFE TURNS FROM BLACK TO GRAY
   YOU AND I LAY TIGHT AND OLD
I WILL LOOK UPON YOU
   AND HOLD YOUR HAND
STILL THANKFUL - STILL GRAND

IN THE STILLNESS OF THE MORNING
   IN THE FRESH FALLEN SNOW
THOUGH THE BABIES HAVE GROWN
   I'LL STILL LOVE YOU

1987

WE WERE QUIET

Oh the racing thoughts
*   that needed to be quiet*

But the 'what if's' ran the 100 yard dash
*   across my heart*
*   couldn't they be quiet*

Oh but for the moment
*   quiet is so hard for the insecure*
*   so taxing for the do-it-yourself man*
*   quiet is the only thing*
*   I can do nothing about*

*   we were quiet and I screamed*
*   a silent scream to be heard —*
*   help me Lord Jesus*
*   to be quiet and hear*

1987

ON THE PASSING OF GRANDPA

"is a man the accumulation of his life's events?"
- line from eulogy

Is there another side to grumpy old men?
I think so
Grandpa, you were a strong wood worker
with a tongue as sharp as your whittling knife
slice and carve - cut the corners
make the point or is it - give the point?

Aging is tough for everybody though
all the tension of life mixed with just enough pain
or is that aches and pains? I forget
must be old age - oops - I said it -
darn aging process
or is it all you ever wanted to say coming out
through false teeth?
got me? - or should I say - got you!

I had my eyes fixed
I kept seeing old people everywhere I looked
I lost focus on the people part
and got overwhelmed by the old -

Whatever - Goodbye Grandpa - I enjoyed you -
sometimes

1996

IN THE MIST

Running for a touch
your hair - your beauty
on my fingertips is enough
to thrill me

In the mist, just ahead of
comfort from the pain
some call life - some lessons
are harder than others
to get down - GULP

In the mist just ahead of
a place to hide with you
like those precious moments
in secret - hiding in the dark
whispering to each other - no one heard
or even if they did -
WHO CARES!

In the mist all around me
sticking to me -
life giving moisture
beyond anyone's sight
I have no fog lamps - I need none
"Blessed are those who have not seen
and yet believe"

1996

THIS BED

This bed is so small a place
        so small a place
to live the amount of life
        we live on it

Like a patch
        on a large colorful quilt
One small square in a great pattern
        of gold and gray, blue and brown

Life all around
        art and design
        joy and sorrow
A time for every season
        in a place so small

1996

happy green eyes

loves runs deep
and is woven of differences
sandy blonde hair
child like sighs
late night goodbyes
and a slightly cold nose

love flies high
and lives in a small room
with a second story cross
a hand to dream with
a women to grow with
and my Lord
to find guidance with

love is life
and grows in all
i give my all
to Jesus Christ
He gives me all
in happy green eyes
my world blooms
with rainbow colors
and a princess lover
named Patti

1997

I'VE SEEN ANOTHER SIDE

You've let me see another side
an intimate side of your love
a strong man
now shown weak and frail
vulnerable - I sat and watched
behind the curtains
I saw the tenderness
which gave me life
life in all its glory
the touch of the hand of love
between two in love
with me

thank you
for letting me in, Dad

1996

DAD

you always were
the biggest guy I knew

so big - so strong

I always wanted
to be like you

so big - so strong

I always felt
I couldn't reach high enough
to reach you

You were so big - so strong

but I did try -
sometimes too hard
to understand you

see you were so big - so strong

and now I regret
that we missed so much together

so forgive me
have I become
too big and too strong
for us to love?

your son, joe

1998

from inside

I watched your eyes today

in the cold - walking

through the valley

but the shadow I saw

was not of death

but dreams

families, hopes

children - coming and going

2000

AS IF A DREAM

I HAVE STUMBLED THROUGH THE DARK
TORN - BLOODED FEET
FORCING THEIR WAY TOWARD TOMORROW
I HAVE ACHED
CLAWING UPWARDS TOWARDS THE LIGHT
NO HOPE - A WORN OUT HEART
STILL PUMPING - BARELY ENOUGH LIFE
I HAVE FELT WHAT OTHERS CALLED
'THE REAL WORLD'
AND SOUGHT FOR ANOTHER
A WORLD OF LOVE, PEACE AND PURPOSE

A TALE IS TOLD OF ANOTHER PLACE
ANOTHER KING - A KING OF LOVE AND PEACE
BUT WHO COULD BELIEVE IN THIS TALE
- NOT A VETERAN LIKE ME -
I'VE 'SEEN TOO MUCH' (OR NOT ENOUGH)
I'VE 'FELT TOO MUCH' (OR NOT ENOUGH)
FOR STORIES LIKE THAT

(AS IF A DREAM continued)

BUT EVERY ONCE IN A WHILE THE LITTLE BOY
DREAMS OF THAT PLACE OF LOVE
WHERE PEOPLE HOPE IN GOD
AND GOD MEETS THEM
WITH HIS GREAT ARMS AND HOLDS THEM
CLOSE AS ONLY A GREAT FATHER CAN DO
"YES THE BOY DREAMS"
CRIES THE CYNICAL VETERAN
"BUT WHAT ARE DREAMS TODAY?"

'FAITH IS THE SUBSTANCE OF THINGS
HOPED FOR,
THE EVIDENCE OF THINGS NOT SEEN'

IF THIS IS A DREAM
PLEASE DON'T WAKE ME UP

2003

felt old

worn out   hurt and beat
broken in body   tired in mind

felt old today

forgot what that was
was caught looking
what a word
some things are cool when old
like building - history is old

but old people
freak me out
they have wrinkles
on their wrinkles
is that too much skin?
they stumble and fall
and need help wiping their butts

OLD is the heaviest three letters
that ever chased me
old means death
but some old things go on
like the earth and sky
where does the words faith and old connect?
I have old faith-filled friends who are cool
        everlasting is an old word

2004

more beautiful with age

I heard it said
        many things
        when you add time
        become priceless and more beautiful
        fine wine
        diamonds
        works of art

And in truth
you are much more beautiful now
I have enjoyed watching and experiencing

        the wonder of my wife

2004

I CAUGHT A GLIMPSE

I caught a glimpse of confidence
from your eyes the other day
it jolted me - it challenged me - it excited me
  it brought me peace

Someone of your worth would trust
someone like me with such valuable things
like you and our family

We have come through so much
even though I have led
(thank you for that privilege)
I have always followed our Master

He it is who has done
the good work in us both

2004

I CAN'T BUT TELL

I TRY TO BE STILL

      BUT SOMEONE KEEPS SPEAKING

      'YOU ARE THE NEW CREATION'

I TRY TO BE QUIET

      BUT SOMEONE KEEPS SHOUTING

      'YOU ARE THE PEOPLE OF GOD

      REDEEMED AND MADE RIGHTEOUS'

I TRY TO KEEP IT TOGETHER

      BUT AN EARTH SHATTERING

      PRESENCE KEEPS MOVING

      I CAN'T STAY STILL I'VE GOT TO DANCE

      TO THE GLORY OF A SAVIOR LIKE JESUS

      I AM THE REDEEMED

      THE ONES WHO SAY SO

      THE ONES WHO SHOUT THE PRAISES

I CAN'T BUT TELL

      OF THE GLORIOUS SAVIOR

      AND OF WHAT GOD HAS DONE IN ME

2005

Feelings

feelings are so illusive
>*they run to and fro*
>*like the white rabbit*
>*and I, like Alice, try to catch them*
>*when I do*
>*it's like a pill that makes one*
>*larger and one smaller*

feelings are so illusive
>*they're like the cheshire cat*
>*appearing and vanishing*
>*playing tricks that aren't funny*
>*they're like the mad hatter*
>*driving you crazy*
>*and making no sense*
>*they're like the red queen*
>*demanding the impossible*
>*and ordering someone's head*
>*to be cut off*

feelings are so illusive
>*I'll trust mine to the King*
>*who is the Lord of Lords*

2005

MY ROSE (FOR BRAELYN)

I SAW YOU FIRST - SMALL AND HIDDEN
IN THE GARDEN OF PRAYER
NOT ONE PETAL WAS EXPOSED
YOUR LIFE FLOWING FROM GOD
MAKING A PERFECT BUD
EXCITED AND ACCEPTING I REACHED
TO HOLD THE ANSWERED PRAYER
MY DAUGHTER
WITH EACH DAY - EACH NEW SEASON
I'M WATCHING AS AN EAGER GARDENER
A ROSE COMING FORTH
FROM THAT SMALL HIDDEN BUD
SO MANY SURPRISES
A DANCER, A MUSICIAN
A POET, A WRITER
A LOVELY WOMAN
YOU ARE THAT CHERISHED ROSE
BRAELYN I LOVE YOU
YOUR DAD

2005

(untitled)

a rose
is such a delicate bloom
one wisp of wind
and petals are gone

a rose
is such a delicate beauty
one look
will capture the heart

a rose
invades the senses
directs the air
stimulates the heart

a rose
by any other name
would not be as dear
as you are to me

Brae, you are my rose
   your grateful dad

2005

THE WOMAN I LOVE

so much of what you do thrills me
not just your features
but the way you are

the cute - little girl ways
the cuddle - your smile
the feetzies - the cold nose rub
your love of children

you so complete me
polish off my rough edges
fit so well in my embrace
our faces are one
when our lips meet

I love you now more
than I did at first
I cherish the woman I love

2005

I WOULD LIE WITH YOU

I would lie with you
        in virgin grass
        on summer days
        with skin touching
I would lie with you
        holding each other
        TIGHTLY until danger passes
I would lie with you
        in the cold of winter
        receiving warmth from your body
        feeling your breath on my face
I would lie with you
        and close my eyes
        so I see nothing
        but full imagination, lost in you
I would lie with you
        as the sun sets
        in orange and yellows
            in love

2005

I WILL NOT STAND STILL

I WILL NOT STAND STILL
AND WATCH TOUCHING MOMENTS FLEE
I WILL NOT STAND STILL
WHEN MY ARMS CAN HOLD YOU
I WILL NOT STAND STILL
IN ANGER OR PRIDE
WHEN A SIMPLE MOTION
WOULD TURN EVERYTHING AROUND
I WILL NOT STAND STILL
AND REGRET THE ACTION - WEEPING ALONE
I WILL NOT STAND STILL AND MISS YOU
TIME DOESN'T WAIT FOR THE STILL MAN
AND NEITHER WILL I
I WILL NOT STAND STILL
WITH CLOSED LIPS AND A HARD HEART
AND CURSE WHAT SOMEONE ELSE HAS DONE
I WILL NOT STAND STILL AND BECOME STONE
I WILL SPEAK IN PRAISE
I WILL TOUCH GENTLY WITH RESPECT
        AND HONOR
I WILL HOLD AND BECOME ONE
        WITH YOU AGAIN.

2005

you are like a rocket

you are like a rocket
an electric jolt
sharp - stunning
elusive - alive

you blow me away
I long to be with you
in intimate moments alone
your touch thrills me
I look forward with anticipation
to just seeing you again

this mad, scary thing
called love

2005

EVEN THOUGH YOU PLEASE ME

EVEN THOUGH YOU PLEASE ME
THIS PHRASE DOESN'T GO FAR ENOUGH
FOR THE TRUTH BE KNOWN
YOU NOT ONLY PLEASE ME
BUT YOU DELIGHT ME

PLEASING IS SUCH A DEMANDING WAY
OF EVALUATING A GORGEOUS HUMAN

LIKE YOU

DELIGHT IS FUN AND LIGHT
THIS IS WHAT YOU MAKE ME FEEL
WHEN I'M WITH YOU

DELIGHT IS LIKE THE AIR UNDER ME
AS WE SOAR AMONG THE CLOUDS

DELIGHT IS WHAT YOU ARE TO ME
SO PLEASE MY LOVE
KNOW YOU COMPLETE ME

2005

Beloved Daughter

at times you are such a special blend
of sometimes IRON - at times a feather

so STRONG in crazy situations
like iron under a bridge
before a storm

but oh so fragile like a feather in the wind

sometimes heavy - plowing through
no matter what - yet at times
blown to and fro wondering where
you will land

at times - light and enabled
able to float from place to place
with laughter and joy
like a fountain to this dry land

as iron stands strong ready
to hold the bridge
or a beautiful feather
white, smooth to touch, finds its place
so move forward - my daughter
in all your ways - you nest in my heart

2007

ELLA WINKED

beautiful girl
　　　　come out
　　we all want to
　　marvel at you
　　wonderful - wonderful girl

your mom waits
　　and rubs you from outside
your dad
　　talks to you through skin
your grandparents
　　stand on tip-toes
　　holding their breath

Ella
　　you are the result of
　　great teams of love

　　and Ella saw light
　　smiled and winked

2007

poems need no names

poems need no names
attached to draw attention
like gnats that get in your eyes

poems are pure - undefiled
          emotion floating
words, looking for some soul
to refresh and move
          to feel again
like pebbles from the shore

oh for the book that just collects them
what use are pebbles to the child who collects?
they are dreams that shine
and tell of far off lands of adventure
they are shining mysteries that inspire

commerce and words of life
          get too confused
the color green is for trees and grass
new life springing up in verse
poems as rich as wild flowers
pages and pages of wonder

so write o poet
let the songs of word-feelings come to bless

2007

you are the person
people write poems for

your hair inspires words of passion
as it flows through my hands
your skin milks phrases from my heart
as I draw it over mine
your eyes let deep yearning swim
off lips that kiss them
your lips join with my whole being
as we embrace and are lost in joy
your body is an ocean of delight
to my mind and hands
always open and inviting
your feet stand next to mine
as we embrace facing love

2007

TINY BOY

WITHIN EACH MAN
      A SMALL BOY LIVES
THERE IS FEAR IN HIS EYES
AND HIS BACK IS AGAINST THE WALL
HE CROUCHES
      WAITING   WAITING

      WAITING TO BE LOVED
      HELD AND SPOKEN TO
      WITH WORDS OF TENDERNESS

YES AS MEN GROW
      THEY FEEL THEIR STRENGTH
      THEY TRY HARD TO FORGET
        THE TINY BOY
THEY SCOLD HIM FOR CRYING
THEY TRY TO STOP HIM FROM FEELING
THEY THREATEN AND LAUGH AT HIS REQUESTS

      BUT THAT TINY BOY
STILL WAITS AND EVERY ONCE IN AWHILE
BREAKS THROUGH AGAIN
YES HE IS PUSHED BACK INTO THE CORNER
AND YELLED AT AND TOLD 'SHUT UP ALREADY'

(TINY BOY continued)

THERE WAS A BOY WHO CRIED OUT
AND A LOVING GRACIOUS GREAT FATHER
CAME AND HELD THE BOY
>UNTIL HIS TEARS STOPPED
>AND HIS TREMBLING CEASED
>THE BOY WENT WITH HIS DADDY
>AND RECEIVED THE HEALING LOVE
>>HE ALWAYS NEEDED

"SUFFER NOT THE LITTLE BOYS
TO COME UNTO ME, FOR SUCH
IS THE KINGDOM OF GOD"
>JESUS OF NAZARETH

2007

VALENTINE TIES

cards, candy and more cards

    they're nice

    but I believe

    Valentine's day is about ties

    (not bow ties or straight ties)

but emotional ties

bonding one to another

    Jesus ties

(not that He wore one)

    forever ties

that hold two people together

through thick and thin - good and bad

richer or poorer

until - forever

'Bless be the tie that binds

all hearts in Christian love'

I am grateful for our tie

I love you now and forever

    Happy Valentine's Day

2007

I have no reasons

I have no reasons
  to explain the love
      I have for you

I've made lists
  and they tell no story
      of the love I have for you

for if you were or did
  none of the things on those lists
      I would still love you

love is mysterious
  it grabs your heart
      opens it up to let another in

love is wonderful and boundless
  'love is of God
      and those who love are born of God
          and know God'
              I John 4:7-8

2007

QUIET   PLEASE

STOP   THE   CHATTER

the clattering

clattering

clattering

CHAT ——— TER

'you talk so much - you even worry my pet'

STOP THE DIARRHEA OF WORDS

oh to listen and hear

a still small voice

spoken to those who have ears

to hear

2007

I WANTED A PICTURE

I wanted a picture of you
that excited me
so I looked for the perfect moment
in a flash I had it
but it was too small to fill all you are
you are a collage
of great and beautiful moments
throughout the years
thank you for the photo album
in my heart

Love upon you
Always
Joe

2007

'ON 30'

we have walked
through life's stuff
and we still reach
for each other's hand
I want to
there is a desire
to be with you

this love is a great mystery
almost crazy
but so real
for a guy into truth
it is staggering to realize
that for thirty years
from the 'I DO' day
you have brought me joy

I want to thank you
Your grateful husband

2007

cynical

what a catch word
so hip   so chic
always intellectual
like a slogan on a chain
hung around my neck
entertaining
we must be entertained
hate the silence
it scares me into feeling
something besides life-less consumerism
thought I'd write
another poem or song
so you could spend
more bucks
on my obsession

2008

I felt divorced

I was apart from you

I felt divorced

I was lonely

and spoke to the walls

I was lonely

I wore your sweatshirt

had visions of every inch of you

yet couldn't reach or touch

I felt cut off

the knife was cold and sharp

it cut the 'we' from my heart

I stood bleeding - waiting for you

fighting legions of despair

2008

like teenagers

We were driven with passions
    yearnings of love
    we couldn't wait to hold each other
    with intimate embraces
    too in love to speak
We fumbled with clothing
    but didn't care who heard
    the sounds of our love
    again and again
    we filled ourselves with ourselves
    'til exhausted we forgot
    the time, the place, how old we were
We merely fell asleep
    smiling in each others arms
    'til tomorrow

2008

my one true love

you are a world unto me

a frolic away

away - away

I go - forgetting the day

lost in you

as my fingers touch you

the source of healing pleasure

I do not want to return

do we have to let others into the room?

to break the embrace of

my one true love

do I know you or am I known by you?

or does it matter when we are together?

who knows? - kiss me

hold me until the world fades

into sighs that chase this day away

so I lie with

my one true love

('my one true love' continued)

I stay in this paradise

for who knows how long

I forget the years before

they aren't as important as the now

and besides I've cast them aside

knowing they do not compare

with the excitement

of spending another moment with

my one true love

I stumble for words

to say what is in my heart

I see only you

my one true love

2008

CANDLE

the candle before lit
is in darkness
> quiet

then a spark
that ignites the wick
light - powers out darkness
no longer quiet
as the dancing flame illuminates
creates shadows
burns bright

as the time goes
so goes the wick
and wax flows
creating shapes on the sides
the wick grows ever shorter

until in a pool of wax
it drowns
it's light out
as the thing that held it firm
now gone
is what entombs the flame
until darkness again covers all
> quiet

2008

YOU HAVE GIVEN ME
A LOVE STORY FOR MY LIFE

IN THIS WORLD
WITH SO MUCH TRAGEDY AND PAIN
SO MANY SHIPS CRASHED ON ROCKS
OF SELFISHNESS AND PRIDE

YOU GAVE ME
A LOVE STORY
FOR MY LIFE

WHAT A FANTASTIC STORY
YOU AND I WRITE
AS WE WORK AND LOVE
OUR WAY THROUGH EACH CHAPTER
EACH SEASON - NEW
EACH DAY - BLESSED

MY GRATITUDE IS YOUR INVITATION TO ME
I AM HONORED TO WRITE AND READ
OUR LOVE STORY TOGETHER

2009

BETHESDA
(JOHN 5:2-9)

you are to me - Bethesda
a pool of still refreshing water
that I can dip my body in
sensing healing

often I sit next to you
waiting for you to move
unto my own disease

God knew what water could refresh
thrill and cool me
so He showed me - you
my Bethesda
in the midst of my dry and busy world

thanx

2009

I WILL REGRET

I will regret
the days lost
when we depart

I know we will meet
on golden streets
but I do not know
if you will realize
the great love
I'll still have for you

even if I pass first
I will still miss you
if you go before
I will still hunger
for your embrace

it's all so confusing to me
so worldly but
I love you and want to dance
with you forever

2009

Isaiah 40

running to catch - WHAT?
running to catch - LIFE
it's running out - that scares me

I can't run any faster - I tire
I need rest only God can give
His speed is best
even youths grow weary and tired
and young men fall exhausted

set the speed and course
O Creator of the wind
I run on

2009

another graven image

like shadows
> *printed on paper*
> *people here today*
> *and gone tomorrow*
> *moments trapped*
>> *to remind forgetting memories*
> *of what was or was not*
> *frozen smiles that today are gone*

graven images
> *to help or to haunt*
> *we who remain to collect*
>> *those views and grieve*

2010

the same disease

stopped to speak with one bleeding
stopped to listen
pain - hurt - anger
what medicine will do?
I don't know how to help
solve the problem - eat the pain
make it go away
I can't - but I'm here

"I lost my soul mate,
she left me - I lost
I met someone else - she only takes
all women are evil" he said

I don't know
how to deal with pain
but I'm here - I hear
let's walk away
and meet again

we can't make the bleeding stop
but we can touch it
and not be afraid
we need to catch the same disease
called being human

2010

THE RAG DOLL PRINCESS

SO LIGHT - SWIRLING
LIKE A FLOWER PETAL IN THE WIND
THAT CAN BE DAMAGED
WITH A STRONG GUST AND CRUSHED

A HEART OF A PRINCESS
CAPTURED BY A LOVER AND STOMPED
UNTIL NO MORE BLOOD OR BEAUTY
CAN BE NOTICED

INSIDE THE BEAUTY
RAVAGED AND DECEIVED BY THE KNIGHT
WHO SHINED NOT AT ALL
TORN AND BROKEN

THE QUESTION EMERGES
CAN A PRINCESS BE RESTORED
OR IS SHE TO LIMP FOREVER
SEEKING WHATEVER IS SUPPOSED TO BE?

IN THE IVORY TOWER
SHE TITLED LOVE
IS SHE TO WANDER LOOKING AND HOPING
TO FIND SOMETHING
TO STOP THE BLEEDING?

{continued}

HEAL THE BEATING
FROM THE HEARTLESS METAL MAN
AND HIS BRUTAL SWORD
WHICH STOLE THE PRINCESS'S
INNOCENSE?

IN ONE BOLD MOVE
THE IDYLLIC DREAM OF ROMANCE
NOW WANDERING TO FIND ANOTHER
TO SAVE AND HEAL - DESIRE HER ALONE

HAS SHE LOST HOPE?
WILL SOMEDAY HER PRINCE COME?
IS IT ALL JUST MADNESS
TO MOVE TO THIS SONG
LIKE LOVE STARVED PUPPETS?

ONLY THE RAG DOLL PRINCESS
CAN DECIDE TO GO ON SINGING

2010

GROWING UP

the minute you ask
if she is grown
the moment passes
and she already is
before my eyes
in a twinkle
the girl is now a lady
grown and beautiful
ready to leave
and join to another
when did it happen?
in the times
when we are asking the questions
fly on blackbird
I pray in wonder and joy

2010

silence

perhaps the deepest sound
is the air
when it is silent

the deepest sigh
is the depth of feeling
when it is silent

I can speak no more
I have opened my soul
to you - in silence

I receive you
hold you
love you
no longer with words
for our love has grown
to the point of
silence

2010

trickle

the other day I stood speaking with someone
light conversation about nothing - YOU KNOW

then I noticed a trickle of blood at their feet
it made me nervous
so I cut the talk session short
and thought 'how weird is that?'

went to someone else and gabbed on
about nothing much - YOU KNOW
how life is - light stuff - fun for all

then a small trickle, actually a puddle
was flowing down their leg
bleeding - hurting wounds
so I gabbed on
never acknowledging their pain

I went home and tried hard to forget
the strange episodes
and as I sat
I noticed a trickle at my feet
tears mixed with blood - my pain
but I stood alone

Is there anything to be learned?
and HE answered 'which one was a
neighbor to the man?'
do YOU KNOW?

2010

wasteland

walking - looking - at the wasteland
mounds and mounds of discarded lives
crushed down

someone built a great big money house
on one of those garbage dumps

damn good looking
but what a smell of greed
and consumerism

hope is the drink of the day
and no one has wine like that
except HIM who makes water
polluted or not into smooth wine
to satisfy the soul

thank you JESUS CHRIST
for those miracle working hands
which will one day
turn our wasteland into golden streets
and a river of hope-wine
flowing through the midst of joy.

2011

MY PRECIOUS BOY

what wonder
you have added
to my life

what lessons God
has taught me
through you

and though you have grown
still images of you
dance and run
through my mind
with delight
pure delight

on this 15th
I will cherish you
and be thankful
for another year

your dad

2011

virginity

you were so pure

so young

a beauty exposed

innocent

trusting

with a gift

so rare

so unique

so precious

that I fumbled

trying to understand

what gentleness was

it slipped through

my fingers

in a moment of passion

I took your virginity

and you gave me back mine

thanks

2011

HIPS

sometimes
　　we disagree
　　　　over whatever

BUT OH YOU'VE GOT SUCH HIPS

sometimes
　　you're in one place
　　　　I'm in another

THE LINES OF YOUR LEGS CONNECT TO (YOU'RE RIGHT) YOUR HIPS

sometimes
　　it's one thing
　　　　after another

BUT THE CURVES YOU HAVE !!!!!!!!

I can be speeding
　　and my mind
　　　　thinks

HIP　　HIP　　HOORAH

This may sound shallow
but after all these years
I'm still excited about your

HIPS

2010

cast away

loneliness
is a deep strange creature
it wraps its tentacles
around your heart
your mind
your body
even into your bones
cold waves crashing over you
cold waves crashing over you
as you hold onto your bed
night after starless night
adrift
cast away

thank you
you've rescued me from that creature
by being in my bed

2011

affirmation

you've brought me to my knees

your love has overwhelmed me

I'm weak in your arms

I struggle without you to hold

and yet there is a confidence

as Jesus brings us together

an affirmation of His love

found in your arms

thanks

2011

kathy

they say there is a land of giants
who use small people to their gain
beatings are common
for reasons known only to
those hideous creatures

you and I dwelt in that land for many years
I always wished it was only a nightmare
because rescuing from giants
is a very hard business

you got so scared - I got so scared
I couldn't speak - couldn't yell
I wanted to so badly - but I left you alone
I had to leave - find my somewhere to hide

I felt so little - so weak - so intimidated
so in horror I watched - as you were beat
as the giant beat on you
I was too small to help - hidden but not safe

not once did I run and let you down
but many times - left you abandoned
you struggled on alone
you are the brave one

I wanted to cry
but didn't think anyone would come
see the lady of the house
loved to urge the giant on
teasing him with her selfish ways
it was so sick
awash in tears, puke and pain

what was right or wrong?
I've stopped thinking
> *but not of you - kathy.*

2011

roses on silk

the way you hold
your legs
as you slide silk up
over your thigh

the way silk
caresses your body
as I slide my hand
up your leg

why hold back
the moment is given to us
like silk to the skin
like roses to the scent

the way you slowly
take it off
I enjoy looking
at the way you hold
your legs inviting me
into love
smooth
as silk

2011

carpe diem

we're watching
each other get old
looking for wrinkles
and crows feet
wondering how much
flabby skin we have
or what dye or surgery
we've used to fight time
as it passes us by
      my question - WHY?

      life is now
      my brother
      carpe diem

2011

with you

I'd spend a moment
alone with you
my first moment
my last moment
in your embrace
all other things
seem meaningless
when I'm with you
my love flows freely
comfort and peace
is found with you

if friends or family
ask where I am?
tell them
I'm with you

2012

(untitled)

without touching you
        I live in a land of urges
unfulfilled desires
        cut off from life

without touching you
        I dwell in a land of shadows
        disconnected
reaching but never grasping
        love

without touching you
        I am alone
love is only a mere concept
        to think about
pondering the wonder
        of touching you
        my love

2012

You - and the man I am

You
have helped build
the man I am

You
have polished
and chipped the stones

You
have soothed
have smoothed the edges

You
with your grace
and love have washed and worked

You
have sweat and prayed
believing the vision

You
have appreciated and admired
the man I have become

2012

THE SNAKE IN BLACK

THAT SNAKE RAISED HIS HEAD AGAIN
IN A WHISPER LIKE CAIN AND EVE

SWEET BABIES
ONE BULLET AFTER ANOTHER
WAS IT THE GUN?
OR THE CRAZY?
OR THE SNAKE BEHIND IT?

TOO MUCH   TOO MUCH
TOO MUCH BLOOD
THE POLITICIANS RUN
AND THE SNAKE IN BLACK
HAS WON AGAIN

WE LOOK FOR ANSWERS
AND ARE BLIND TO IT ALL
THIS SPIRIT ROAMS FREE
POSSESSING MINDS IN DELICATE WAYS
BUT LIKE CAIN

WE ARE QUITE SURPRISED
WHEN WE KILL
TOO MUCH   TOO MUCH
FEED THE SNAKE IN BLACK THE CHILDREN
TOO MUCH BLOOD

THE NRA HAS STRINGS TO PULL
MONEY TO FEED THE SNAKE
GUNS DON'T KILL PEOPLE - BULLETS DO
AND STILL THE SNAKE PULLS

WHEN WILL WE WAKE UP
AND TURN TO THE ONE
WHO CUTS THE HEAD OFF
OF THE SNAKE IN BLACK

- AFTER NEWTOWN, CT

2012

YOU STAYED

OUR YOUTH
FELL OFF THE BUS
LIKE UNCLAIMED LUGGAGE
OUR LUGGAGE WAS GONE
BUT YOU STAYED

I WENT CRAZY AGAIN
RODE ON TOP OF CABS
DANCED NAKED IN FOUNTAINS
BUT YOU STAYED

I WAS BITTER
AND LASHED OUT
WITH FOOLISH WORDS
THAT I SHOULD NEVER HAVE SAID
BUT YOU STAYED

('YOU STAYED' continued)

I SPOKE OF DREAMS
THAT MARTIANS TOLD ME
I WAS SCARED AND BROKEN
BUT YOU STAYED

YOU FORGOT WHO YOU WERE
AND DRIBBLED WITH CONFUSION
COULDN'T EAT
KISSED DEATH ON THE LIPS
IN FEAR
BUT YOU STAYED

IN THE END
I HELD YOUR HAND
YOU WENT AWAY
AND I STAYED

- for mom

2017

in her presence

I awaken to see
   this lovely one
my friend
   but a beauty
  who takes my breath away
so gentle
   yet so strong
   so lovely
   yet so near
so willing
   yet reserved
so right
   to be in her presence

2017

SMALL SIGN

I SAW A SMALL SIGN TODAY

IT SAID "CANCER GONE … ENGAGED"

I DROVE FURTHER

AND THERE IT WAS AGAIN

"CANCER GONE … ENGAGED"

AND I WONDERED

WHO PUT THAT UP AND

WHO WAS IT FOR?

IT WASN'T FOR ME BUT I SAW IT

IT BROUGHT A ROMANTIC SMILE

AND A WARM CARESS TO MY HEART

IT INSPIRED ME

TO LEAVE SOME SMALL SIGNS

ON MY ROAD

2018

SHALLOW

tiny images on a large screen
she stands waiting - young and free
loud screams
to make it more intense
more smoke
show the crash again and again
she stands ready
to dive off the TOWER

it was the end of the world
in technicolor
to float and soar
into the reflection of death

wide screen
(buy a bigger screen
if you want to
see more and feel less)
they said
"it was too shallow"

tiny images
on a large screen

2018

why poems?

why do I write poems?
i really do not write them
they flow out of me
like water backed up
> *a release of emotion*
and they are called poems

simply words
letters linked together
ink on a page
nothing really
good or bad
just a flow
> *going somewhere*

2018